The ABC's of Asthma

An Asthma Alphabet Book
for Kids of All Ages

By
Kim Gosselin

Published by
JayJo Books, LLC.
Valley Park, MO

A IS FOR ASTHMA.

Wheeze

The ABC's of Asthma

Copyright © 1998, by Kim Gosselin.
First Edition. All rights reserved. No part of this book may be reproduced in
any manner whatsoever without written permission from the publisher.
For information address JayJo Books, LLC., P.O. Box 213, St. Louis, MO
63088-0213. Printed in the United States of America.

Published by
JayJo Books, LLC.
P.O. Box 213
St. Louis, MO 63088-0213

Library of Congress Cataloging-in-Publication Data
Gosselin, Kim
The ABC's of Asthma/Kim Gosselin – First Edition
Library of Congress Catalog Card Number 98-65125
1. Juvenile/Non-Fiction/Health-Related

ISBN 1-891383-04-3
Library of Congress

Special Books for Special Kids ® is a registererd trademark of JayJo Books, LLC.

*The opinions expressed in **The ABC's of Asthma** are those solely of the author. Asthma care is
highly individualized. One should **never** alter asthma care without first consulting a member of the
individual's professional asthma medical team.

GOOD JOB!

I hope you have had fun learning __The ABC's of Asthma.__
Thanks for being my very special friend!

Y IS FOR YOU.

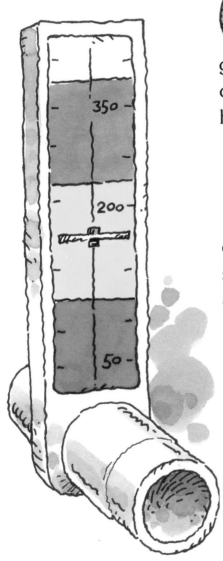

GREEN means my asthma is in good control (HOORAY)!!! I should keep doing everything my doctor and family has told me!

YELLOW means an asthma episode might be starting. My family should still call my asthma doctor and do exactly what they are told.

RED means my asthma needs help. I need to take my asthma medicine right away (and call my doctor).

Z IS FOR ZONE.

Z is for **ZONE**. A lot of peak-flow meters (like mine) have a color zone. The color zone has three different colors, like a stop light: Red, Yellow, and Green. Each color on my peak-flow meter means something different.

Y IS FOR YOU.

Y is for **YOU**. You are special! Remember: Nobody can catch asthma from YOU or anyone else! YOU didn't do anything wrong to cause your asthma, and it's NOBODY'S fault! You are a normal kid who just happens to have asthma.

X IS FOR X-RAY.

X is for **X-RAY**. If my
asthma makes me
get really, really sick (like if I ever have
to go to the hospital), my doctor might want to see an X-ray
of my lungs. An X-ray is just like a picture. Getting an
X-ray doesn't hurt and usually only takes a few seconds!

W IS FOR WHEEZE.

W is for **WHEEZE**. Sometimes having asthma starts my breathing to make a wheezing or whistling sound come from my lungs. When this happens, my family should call my asthma doctor right away!

V IS FOR VISIT TO THE DOCTOR.

V is for **VISIT** to the doctor. My
asthma doctor is like a "best friend"
when it comes to my asthma. The doctor helps me to keep
my asthma in good control. I can talk to them about my
asthma "feelings" too.

U IS FOR UNDERSTANDING FEELINGS.

U is for **UNDERSTANDING** feelings. Sometimes having asthma makes me feel sad, mad, or angry. It can help to talk about having asthma. Talking about my asthma feelings can help me feel better about many things.

T IS FOR ASTHMA TRIGGER.

T is for asthma **TRIGGER**. An asthma trigger is something that might help cause an asthma episode. It's probably something my body is allergic to. Some asthma triggers are: pollen (from grass, trees, or flowers), mold (that grows during damp or rainy weather), certain kinds of foods (like milk, wheat, or peanuts), animal fur, hair, dander, and dust mites.

Non-allergic triggers are infections and exercise.

S IS FOR SPACER.

S is for **SPACER**. A spacer is something that works together with my inhaler. Inhalers and spacers fit together (kind of like a puzzle). Spacers come in many different shapes and sizes. They help get my asthma medicine deep into my lungs (where it works best).

R IS FOR RECORD BOOK.

R is for **RECORD** book (or asthma diary). Whenever I blow air into my peak-flow meter, my family helps me write down the number in my record book. This helps my doctors and nurses decide how much asthma medicine my body needs.

Q IS FOR QUICKLY.

Q is for **QUICKLY**. If the number on my peak-flow meter is too low, I need to get asthma medicine into my lungs very, very quickly (and call my doctor, of course).

P IS FOR PEAK-FLOW METER.

P is for **PEAK-FLOW METER**. A peak-flow meter is a special "tool" to help me measure how open my airways (bronchial tubes) are to my lungs.

O IS FOR DOCTOR'S OFFICE.

O is for doctor's **OFFICE**. It's best for me to go for regular asthma checkups at my doctor's office. Doctors (and nurses, too) help me and my family learn how to keep my asthma in good control.

N IS FOR NEBULIZER.

N is for **NEBULIZER**. A nebulizer is a special machine that has asthma medicine in it. I put a little plastic mask over my nose and breathe in my asthma medicine. Sometimes this is called a "breathing treatment."

M IS FOR MEDICINE.

M is for **MEDICINE**. Usually I take different kinds of medicine to help keep my asthma under good control. My asthma medicine can be: liquid on a spoon, an inhaler with a spacer (the spacer helps my medicine go deep into my lungs where it works best), a nebulizer machine, a pill to chew or take with a glass of water, or even a spray to squirt in my nose!

L IS FOR LUNGS.

L is for **LUNGS**. My lungs are the part of my body that helps me breathe. When I have an asthma episode, my lungs can't do what they are supposed to do.

K IS FOR KIDS.

K is for **KIDS**. Lots of kids have asthma. I'm not the only one! Some kids have brown eyes, some have red hair, some have freckles, and some have asthma (like you and me)!

J IS FOR JUST.

J is for **JUST**.
Just because I
have asthma doesn't
mean I can't do almost
everything other kids do! I
listen to my family. I try to do just
what my doctors and nurses tell me. I play and have fun
learning new things. I'm just a regular kid . . . JUST like you!

I IS FOR INHALER.

I is for **INHALER**. An inhaler is something that has special asthma medicine in it. The asthma medicine helps me breathe easier.

H IS FOR HAIR.

H is for **HAIR**. Animal hair or fur can help cause an asthma episode. Animal dander (their dry and flaky skin) can trigger an asthma episode too. Sometimes, it's best NOT to have a furry pet!

G IS FOR GOOD CONTROL.

G is for **GOOD** control. It's important for me and my family to try to keep my asthma in good control. That means learning about and avoiding asthma "triggers," using my peak-flow meter, getting lots of rest, listening to my doctors, and taking my medicine whenever I'm supposed to!

F IS FOR FAMILY.

F is for **FAMILY**. My whole family helps me to take better care of my asthma. We all work together!

E IS FOR EPISODE.

COUGH COUGH

E is for **EPISODE**. An asthma episode is what happens when I can't breathe very well. My chest might hurt or feel very tight. Sometimes I start to cough. I need to use my asthma medicine FAST when I'm having an asthma episode!

B IS FOR BRONCHIAL TUBES.

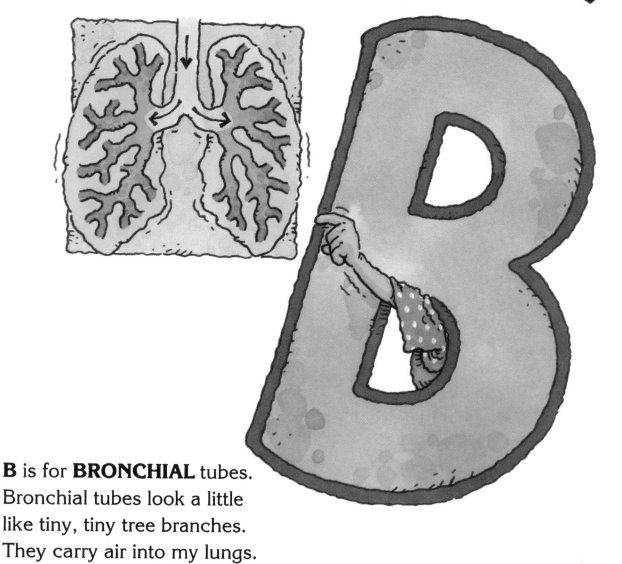

B is for **BRONCHIAL** tubes.
Bronchial tubes look a little
like tiny, tiny tree branches.
They carry air into my lungs.

A is for **ASTHMA**. Having asthma sometimes makes it hard for me to breathe.

Hi Boys and Girls!

<u>The ABC's of Asthma</u> have helped me learn more about asthma. Will you be my special friend and learn **<u>The ABC's of Asthma</u>** with me? Please turn the page to see how our "Asthma Alphabet" begins!

Author's Note

The ABC's of Asthma is my sixth asthma-related children's book. I wrote this particular title because I wanted something very basic from which children could understand and learn. You would be very surprised how many twelve year olds don't know what a "bronchial tube" is! This title can surpass many age ranges, from pre-school through elementary school. I think you will find the text to be informative and the illustrator's pictures fun and entertaining.

Learn lots and have fun!

Kim Gosselin

*This book is dedicated to
my nephew and niece, Alex Andrew and
Jaidyn Danielle. May you always live
happy and healthy lives.
With lots of hugs and kisses, from Aunt Kim*

To order additional copies of The ABC's of Asthma contact your local bookstore or library, or call the publisher directly at (314) 861-1331 or (800) 801-0159.

Write to us at:

JayJo Books, LLC.
P.O. Box 213
Valley Park, MO 63088-0213

Ask about our special quantity discounts for schools, hospitals, and affiliated organizations.
Fax us at (314) 861-2411.

LOOK FOR OTHER BOOKS BY KIM GOSSELIN INCLUDING:

From our *Special Kids in School*® series:

Taking Diabetes to School

Taking Asthma to School

Taking Seizure Disorders to School

And others coming soon!

Others Available Now!

SPORTSercise!
A "School" Story About Exercise-Induced Asthma

Taking Asthma to Camp
A Fictional Story About Asthma Camp

ZooAllergy
A Fun Story About Allergy and Asthma Triggers

Rufus Comes Home
Rufus The Bear With Diabetes™

Taming the Diabetes Dragon
A Fictional Story About Learning to Live Better With Diabetes

and our first large hardcover book: **Smoking STINKS!!**
from our new *Substance Free Kids* ™ series.

Coming in the Spring of 1999!

Taking Food Allergies to School

Taking ADD to School
A Story about Attention Deficit Disorder

Kim Gosselin

ABOUT THE AUTHOR

Kim Gosselin was born and raised in Michigan where she attended Central Michigan University. She began her professional writing career shortly after her two young sons were both diagnosed with chronic illnesses. Kim is extremely committed to bringing the young reader quality children's health education while raising important funds for medical research.

Kim now resides and writes in Missouri. She is an avid supporter of the Epilepsy Foundation of America, the American Lung Association, the American Cancer Society, and a member of the American Diabetes Association, the Juvenile Diabetes Foundation International, the Society of Children's Book Writers and Illustrators, the Small Publishers Association of North America, the Publishers Marketing Association, and The Author's Guild.